A Treasury of
CHRISTMAS SONGS

Twenty-five Favorites to Sing and Play

A Treasury of
CHRISTMAS SONGS
Twenty-five Favorites to Sing and Play

Music arranged and edited by Dan Fox

THE METROPOLITAN MUSEUM OF ART

HENRY HOLT AND COMPANY
New York

All of the works of art reproduced in this book are from the collections of
The Metropolitan Museum of Art.

FRONT COVER DETAIL, TITLE PAGE: *Lune.* Lucien Laforge, French, born 1889, died ?
From an alphabet book published by Henry Goulet, Paris, ca. 1925. Woodcut, printed
in color. Harris Brisbane Dick Fund, 1930 30.96.7

ENDPAPERS: *Snow-laden Pines* (detail). Rockwell Kent, American, 1882–1971. Textile
design in gouache over pencil on board, ca. 1950. Purchase, Leon Lowenstein Foundation Inc. Gift,
1976 1976.536.7

CONTENTS PAGE: *The Adoration of the Magi.* Sano di Pietro (Ansano di Pietro di
Mencio), Italian (Sienese), 1406–1481. Tempera and gold on wood, 11⅞ x 18¾ in.,
ca. 1470. Gift of Irma N. Straus, 1958 58.189.2

BACK FLAP: *Annunciation to the Shepherds.* Pol, Jean, and Herman de Limbourg,
French, active ca. 1400–1416. From *The Belles Heures of Jean, Duc de Berry*;
tempera and gold leaf on parchment, 9⅜ x 5⅝ in., ca. 1410. The Cloisters Collection,
1954 54.1.1 folio 52r

BACK COVER: *The Annunciation* (detail). Sandro Botticelli (Alessandro di Mariano
Filipepi), Italian (Florentine), 1444/45–1510. Tempera and gold on wood,
7½ x 12⅜ in. Robert Lehman Collection, 1975 1975.1.74

Published by The Metropolitan Museum of Art, New York, and Henry Holt and
Company, LLC, 115 West 18th Street, New York, New York 10011.
Distributed in Canada by H. B. Fenn and Company Ltd.

First Edition
Printed in China
13 12 11 10 09 08 07 06 05 04   5 4 3 2 1

Produced by the Department of Special Publications, The Metropolitan Museum
of Art: Robie Rogge, Publishing Manager; Christine Gardner, Editorial Supervisor;
Anna Raff, Designer; Gillian Moran, Production Associate.
All photography by The Metropolitan Museum of Art Photograph Studio unless
otherwise noted.

Text by Carolyn Vaughan

Visit the Museum's Web site: www.metmuseum.org
Visit Henry Holt's Web site: www.henryholt.com

ISBN (MMA): 1-58839-112-4
ISBN (Holt): 0-8050-7657-3   EAN (Holt): 978-0-8050-7657-8

Library of Congress Control Number: 2004102201

Contents

A Note on the Music

In arranging the music for this book, the aim has been simplicity and clarity. All the selections are suitable for beginning to intermediate musicians and each is accompanied by guitar chords. A fingering chart for all of the chords appears at right.

When the piano arrangement is in a key that is awkward for the guitar, capo instructions and alternate chords are given. After the capo is in place, the songs should be played using the chords that appear in parentheses.

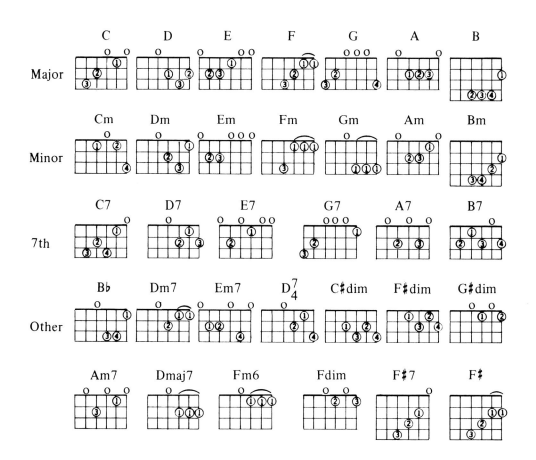

Detail of a postcard. Wiener Werkstätte, Austrian, founded 1905.

At Christmastime, there is truly a song in the air and music all around us—professionals appear in Handel's *Messiah* and children in school holiday concerts; choirs sing at special church services and choral groups perform at the mall; neighbors carol from house to house and rarely seen relatives harmonize by the fireside. Singing seems to be the perfect way to mark this holiday that celebrates family, festivity, and faith.

Christmas carols have been sung at least since the Middle Ages, when they were used with mystery plays to teach the story of the Nativity. Some carols developed from folk songs or from festive drinking and feasting tunes. In the nineteenth century, several English and American poets and members of the clergy added to the repertoire of songs, sometimes matching their own words to existing traditional or classical melodies. Even in contemporary times, catchy popular tunes about snow or reindeer or Santa Claus have become part of the Christmas canon.

"Carol" originally meant a kind of round dance accompanied by singing, and many carols still tend to be simple, lilting tunes that lift the heart and the spirit. Some Christmas songs recount the Bible story so that we can hear again and again about the angels, the shepherds, and the Wise Men. Others are lullabies, re-creating the atmosphere of peace, stillness, and love that surrounded the infant Jesus lying in the manger.

In art, too, the story of the Nativity and scenes of the Virgin and child are among the most popular of subjects, for masters from Gerard David to François Boucher. Other artists, such as William Glackens and Grandma Moses, also are enticed to depict scenes of wintry charm or holiday merrymaking, and a few have even attempted to capture on paper the likeness of Saint Nicholas himself. Within this book, a host of delightful Christmas images accompanies twenty-five favorite songs of the season. So gather around the piano (those who are tone deaf can look at the pictures), "follow me in merry measure," and sing of Yuletide treasure, with this, *A Treasury of Christmas Songs*.

Detail of a postcard. Carl Krenek, Austrian, 1880–1948.

Angels We Have Heard on High

French traditional

This jubilant eighteenth-century French carol vividly conveys what it must have sounded like when a multitude of the heavenly host suddenly began praising God, their song reverberating throughout the countryside. The Bible says that the angels went away after their announcement to the shepherds, but most representations of the Nativity show them hovering over the babe in the manger, continuing their songs of praise.

1. An - gels we have heard on high, Sweet - ly sing - ing
2. Shep - herds, why this ju - bi - lee? Why your joy - ous
3. Come to Beth - le - hem and see Him whose birth the

o'er the plains, And the moun - tains in re - ply,
strains pro - long? What the glad - some ti - dings be,
an - gels sing. Come a - dore on bend - ed knee

(continued on page 12)

The Nativity (detail). Gerard David, Netherlandish, ca. 1455–1523.

Angels We Have Heard on High

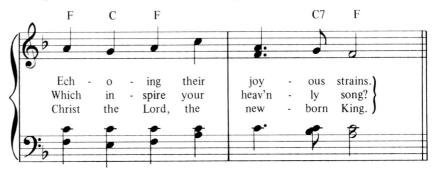

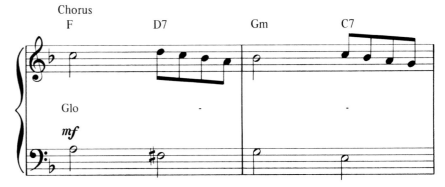

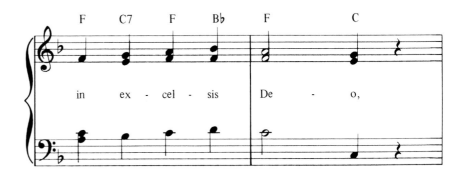

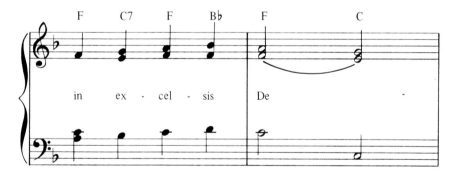

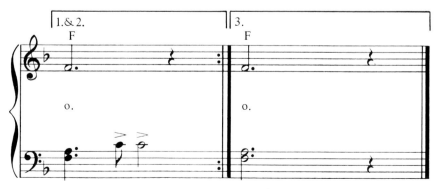

Angel (detail). Aubrey Beardsley, British, 1872–1898.

Auld Lang Syne

Words by Robert Burns
Music Scottish traditional

"Auld lang syne" means "old times" or "the good old days," and it has become the custom to sing this song on New Year's Eve, a time to reflect on the past before moving on to the future. In Scotland, Burns's homeland, holiday revelry and folklore centered on New Year's, called Hogmanay. The Scots still hope—or ensure—that the first person to enter their house at Hogmanay is a tall, dark-haired man, bringing good luck in the coming year.

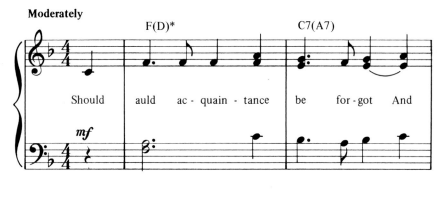

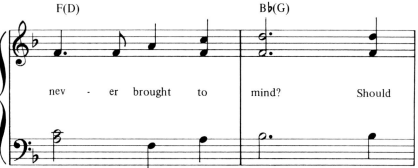

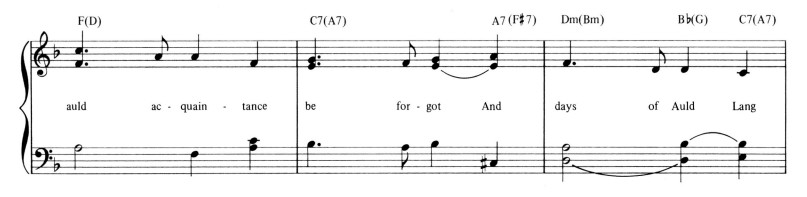

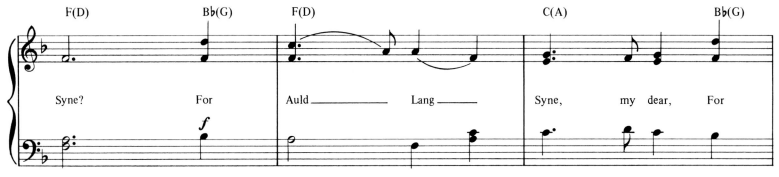

*Guitar: Capo 3rd fret   *Central Park, Winter: The Skating Pond* (detail). Published by Currier and Ives, American, 1857–1907; designed by Charles Parsons, American, 1821–1910.

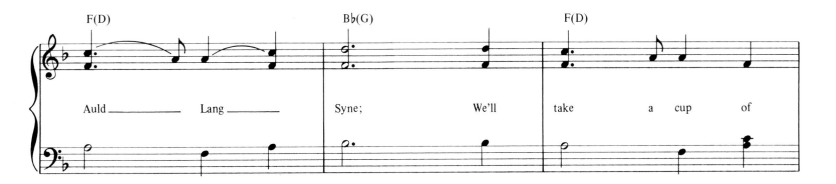

Auld _____ Lang _____ Syne; We'll take a cup of

kind - ness yet For Auld _____ Lang _____ Syne.

Away in a Manger

Words American traditional
Music by James R. Murray

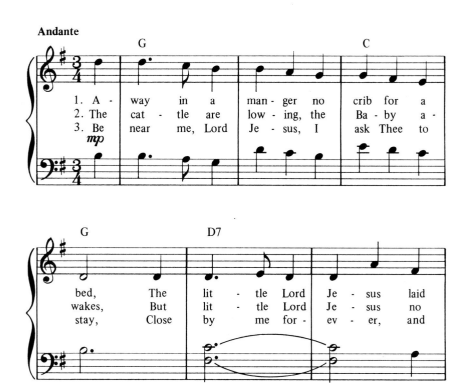

These sweet lyrics were written for children, and the carol evokes the tenderness we feel when gazing at a tiny baby. The artist of this German stained-glass panel clearly took the idea of "manger" seriously. Jesus is lying in a bed of flower-spangled hay that is apparently so fresh and tempting that the donkey, one of the animals traditionally present at the birth of Christ, can't resist taking a mouthful of it.

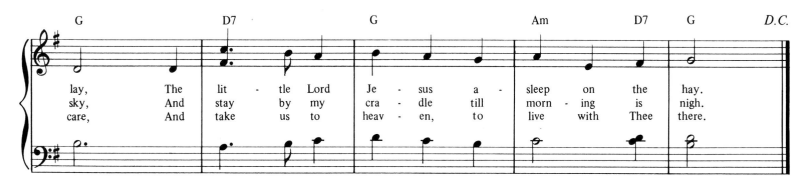

The Nativity (detail). German,
Boppard-on-the-Rhine,
Carmelite Church, 1445.

17

Deck the Halls

Welsh traditional

Even the ancient Romans and early Germanic and Celtic peoples decked their halls with greenery at their midwinter festivals, for evergreens are a natural reminder that life and vegetation are continuing, even when the earth seems bleak and barren. For Christians, holly is also a symbol of Jesus' resurrection. Holly's shiny green and bright red are probably the source of the traditional colors of Christmas, and happily it rhymes with "jolly."

Brightly, with spirit

1. Deck the halls with boughs of hol - ly,
2. See the blaz - ing Yule be - fore us,
3. Fast a - way the old year pass - es,

Fa la la la la la la la la la.

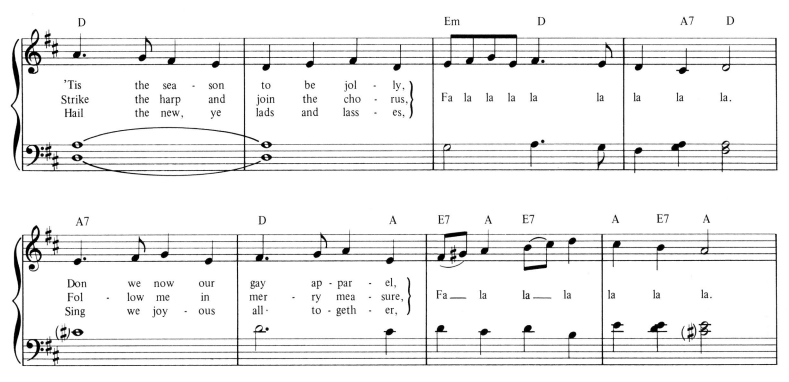

'Tis the sea - son to be jol - ly,
Strike the harp and join the cho - rus,
Hail the new, ye lads and lass - es,

Fa la la la la la la la la.

Don we now our gay ap - par - el,
Fol - low me in mer - ry mea - sure,
Sing we joy - ous all · to - geth - er,

Fa — la la — la la la la la.

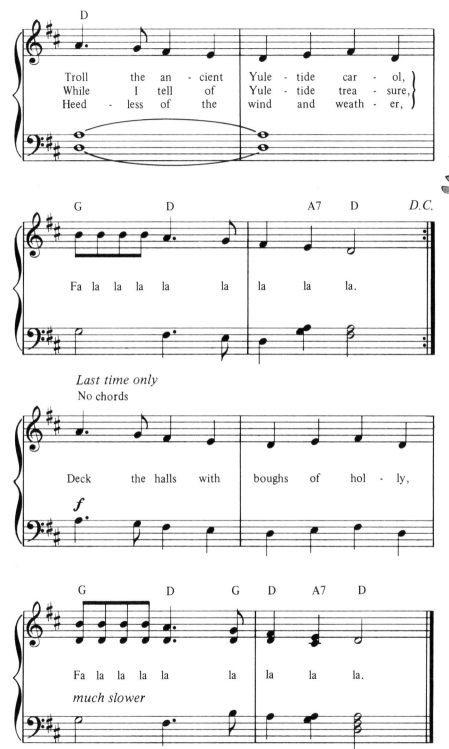

Troll   the an - cient   Yule - tide car - ol, ⎫
While   I tell   of   Yule - tide trea - sure, ⎬
Heed - less of the   wind and weath - er, ⎭

G   D   A7   D   *D.C.*

Fa la la la la   la   la la la.

Last time only
No chords

Deck   the halls   with   boughs of hol - ly,

f

G   D   G   D   A7   D

Fa la la la la   la   la la la.

much slower

Scribner's for Xmas (detail).
Louis Rhead, American, 1857–1926.

The First Noel

English traditional

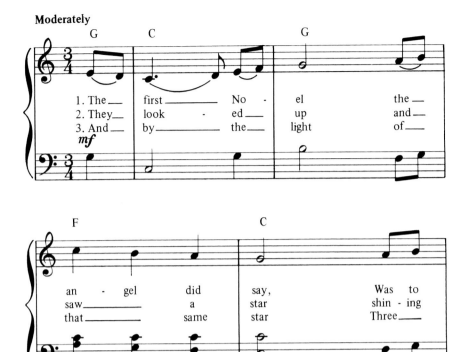

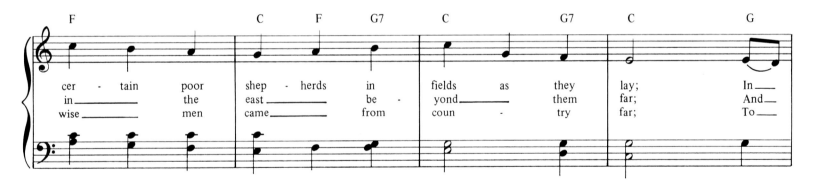

"Noel," or "nowell," probably comes from the Latin word meaning "birth," but it is also related to the French *nouvelles*, meaning "news." Today "noel" can mean a Christmas carol or the news of Christ's birth, like the shepherds heard from "a multitude of the heavenly host," an image magnificently conveyed by the late Baroque Neapolitan crèche figures that adorn the Metropolitan Museum's Christmas tree.

1. The first Noel the angel did say, Was to certain poor shepherds in fields as they lay; In fields where they lay keeping their sheep, On a
2. They looked up and saw a star shining star Was to in the east beyond them far; And it gave great light, And
3. And by the light of that same Three wise men came from country far; To seek for a king it was their in tent, And to

Crèche figures: Nativity with angels and cherubs. Italian (Neapolitan), late 18th–early 19th century.

(continued on page 22)

The First Noel

At left: *Praise of Music* (detail).
Johannes Stradanus,
Netherlandish, 1523–1605.

At right: *The Nativity* (detail).
German, third quarter 15th century.

Chorus

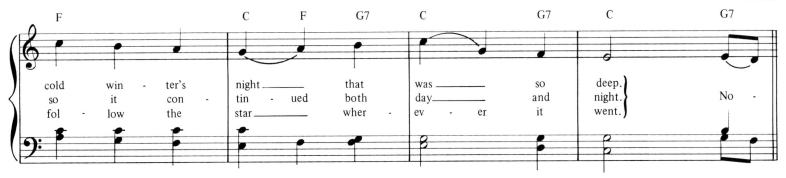

cold win - ter's night_____ that was_____ so deep.
so it con - tin - ued that both day_____ and night.} No -
fol - low the star_____ wher - ev - er it went.}

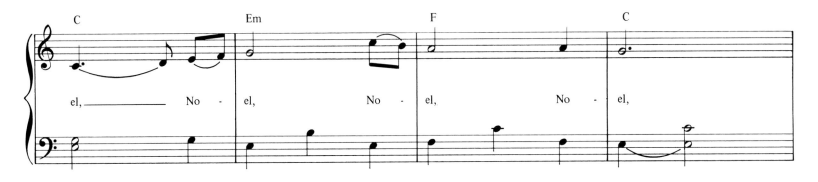

el,_____ No - el, No - el, No - el,

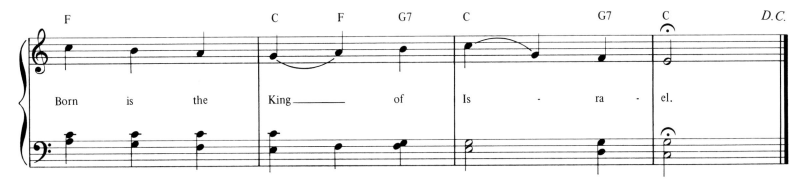

Born is the King_____ of Is - ra - el.

The Friendly Beasts

French or English traditional

A widespread folk belief says that animals gain the power of human speech at midnight on Christmas Eve. An old poem even has them speak in Latin, in phrases that sound charmingly like the noises they actually make: The cock crows "Christus natus est!" ("Christ is born"), while the donkey brays a heehaw-like "Eamus!" ("Let's go!"). In this song, each animal speaks proudly of its gift.

Gently

1. Je - sus our broth - er,
2. "I," said the don - key,
3. "I," said the cow, all

kind and good, was
shag - gy and brown, "I
white and red, "I

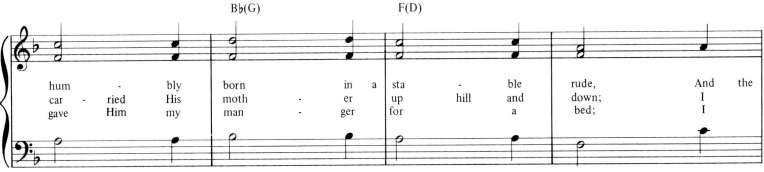

hum - bly born in a sta - ble rude, And the
car - ried His moth - er up hill and down; I
gave Him my man - ger for a bed; I

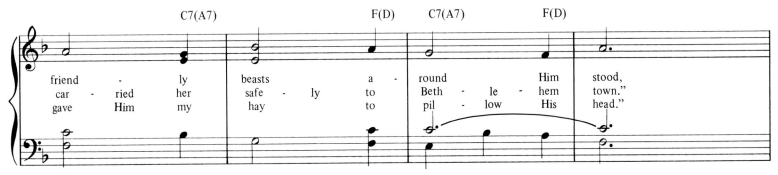

friend - ly beasts a - round Him stood,
car - ried her safe - ly to Beth - le - hem
gave Him my hay to pil - low His

town."
head."

*Guitar: Capo 3rd fret

24

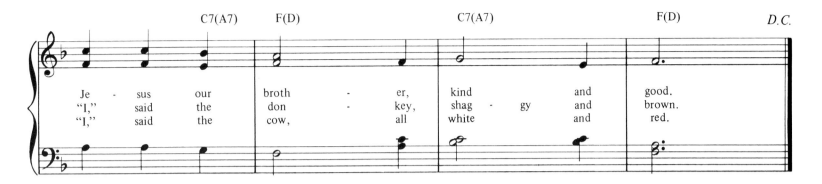

C7(A7)   F(D)   C7(A7)   F(D)   *D.C.*

| Je | - | sus | our | the | broth | - | er, | kind | and | good. |

Je - sus our broth - er, kind and good.
"I," said the don - key, shag - gy and brown.
"I," said the cow, all white and red.

Additional verses:

4. "I," said the sheep with curly horn,
    "I gave Him my wool for His blanket warm;
    He wore my coat on Christmas morn.
    I," said the sheep with curly horn.

5. "I," said the dove from the rafters high,
    "Cooed Him to sleep that He should not cry;
    We cooed Him to sleep, my mate and I.
    I," said the dove from the rafters high.

6. "I," said the camel, yellow and black,
    "Over the desert, on my back,
    I brought Him a gift in the Wise Men's pack.
    I," said the camel, yellow and black.

7. Thus every beast by some good spell,
    In the stable dark was glad to tell
    Of the gift he gave Emmanuel,
    The gift he gave Emmanuel.

The Adoration of the Shepherds (detail).
Marcellus Coffermans, Netherlandish, active 1549–1570.

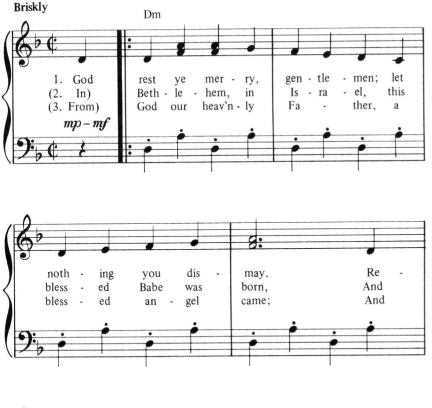

God Rest Ye Merry, Gentlemen

English traditional

May God keep you cheerful," says the first line of this traditional English "luck-visit" song. Such wishes were not appreciated by Ebenezer Scrooge, who is far from merry when he hears these words in Charles Dickens's *A Christmas Carol*: Instead of offering the singer a cup of good cheer, he shoos him away with a ruler.

Christmas-Time, The Blodgett Family (detail). Eastman Johnson, American, 1824–1906.

(continued on page 28)

God Rest Ye Merry, Gentlemen

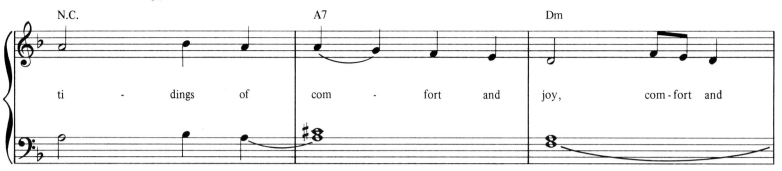

ti - dings of com - fort and joy, com-fort and

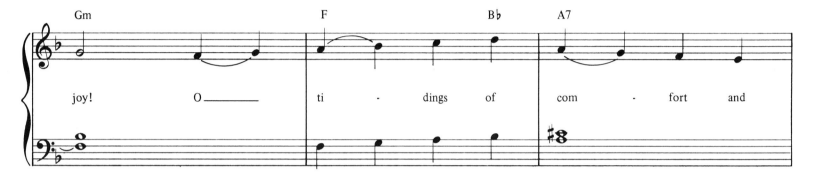

joy! O _____ ti - dings of com - fort and

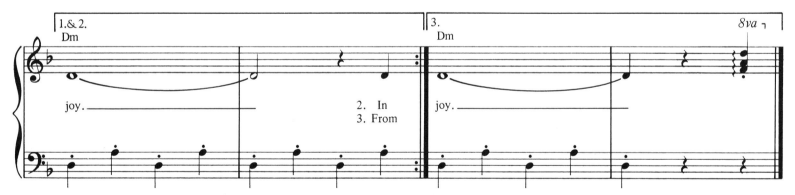

joy. _____ 2. In
3. From

joy. _____

Christmas Visitors (detail).
Randolph Caldecott, British, 1846–1886.

Good King Wenceslas

Words by John Mason Neale
Music traditional

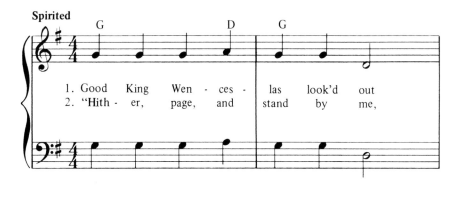

1. Good King Wen - ces - las look'd out
2. "Hith - er, page, and stand by me,

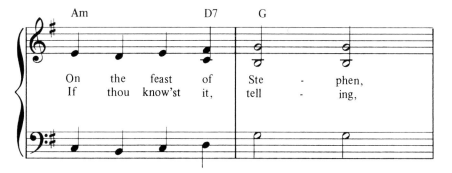

On the feast of Ste - phen,
If thou know'st it, tell - ing,

The Feast of Stephen, or St. Stephen's Day, falls on December 26. In the United Kingdom this date is also celebrated as Boxing Day, a day of gift giving, because it was customary to present small gratuities, or "boxes," to servants and tradespeople. This story of Wenceslas, a tenth-century ruler of Bohemia, is a stirring reminder of the holiday tradition of giving to the less fortunate.

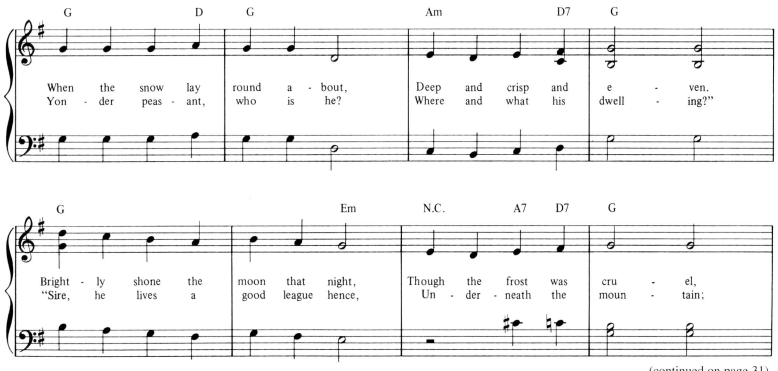

When the snow lay round a - bout, Deep and crisp and e - ven.
Yon - der peas - ant, who is he? Where and what his dwell - ing?"

Bright - ly shone the moon that night, Though the frost was cru - el,
"Sire, he lives a good league hence, Un - der - neath the moun - tain;

(continued on page 31)

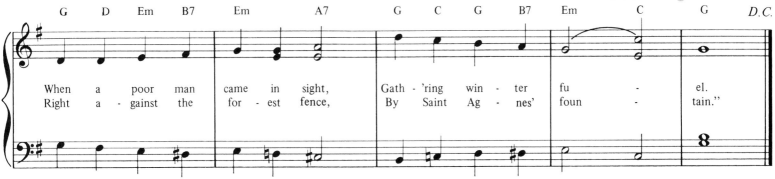

| G | D | Em | B7 | Em | A7 | G | C | G | B7 | Em | C | G | D.C. |

When a poor man came in sight, Gath - 'ring win - ter fu - el.
Right a - gainst the for - est fence, By Saint Ag - nes' foun - tain."

Additional verses:

3. "Bring me flesh and bring me wine,
   Bring me pine logs hither.
   Thou and I will see him dine,
   When we bear him thither."
   Page and monarch forth they went,
   Forth they went together,
   Through the rude wind's wild lament,
   And the bitter weather.

4. "Sire, the night is darker now,
   And the wind blows stronger.
   Fails my heart, I know not how,
   I can go no longer."
   "Mark my footsteps, my good page,
   Tread thou in them boldly.
   Thou shalt find the winter's rage
   Freeze thy blood less coldly."

5. In his master's steps he trod,
   When the snow lay dinted.
   Heat was in the very sod
   Which the saint had printed.
   Therefore, Christian men, be sure,
   Wealth or rank possessing,
   Ye who now will bless the poor,
   Shall yourselves find blessing.

At left: *Old King Cole* (detail). Francis D. Bedford, British, 1864–1934.

Below: *End of the Hunt* (detail). Dale Nichols, American, 1904–1995.

Hark! The Herald Angels Sing

Words by Charles Wesley and
George Whitefield
Music by Felix Mendelssohn

"Angel" comes from the Greek for "messenger," and in the Bible angels often bring God's words to humankind. The original lyrics, by Charles Wesley, the brother of the founder of Methodism, began, "Hark how all the welkin rings," "welkin" meaning "heavens." Whitefield, another poet, amended them to these more fluid lines.

Firmly

1. Hark! the her - ald an - gels sing,_____
2. Hail the heav'n - born Prince of Peace!_____

Glo - ry to the new - born King!
Hail the Son of Right - eous - ness!

Peace on earth and mer - cy mild,_____ God and sin - ners re - con - ciled.
Light and life to all He brings,_____ Ris'n with heal - ing in His wings.

Joy - ful, all ye na - tions rise,_____ Join the tri - umph
Mild He lays His glo - ry by,_____ Born that man no

*Guitar: Capo 3rd fret

(continued on page 34)

Madonna and Child with Saints (detail). Girolamo dai Libri, Italian (Veronese), 1474–1555.

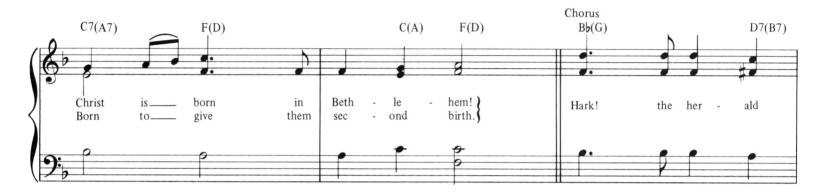

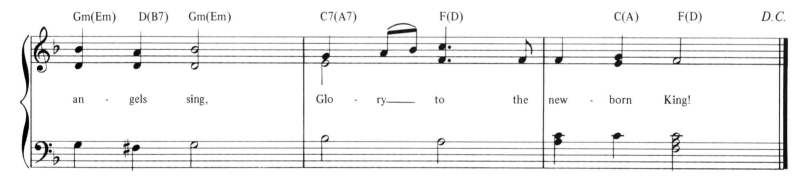

Detail of a postcard. Wiener Werkstätte, Austrian, founded 1905.

Here We Come A-Caroling

English traditional

Joyfully, in 2 (♩. = 1 beat)

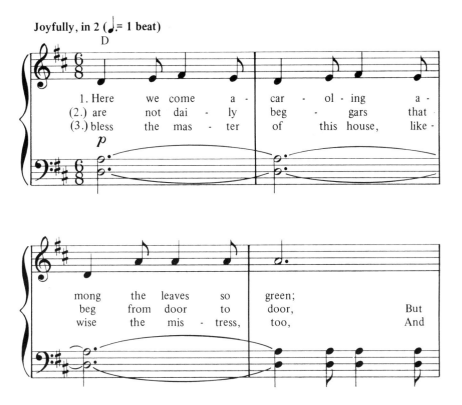

It has long been a tradition for bands of musicians and singers to stroll from door to door at Christmastime. Some carolers offered their songs and good wishes with the hope of a little something in return, while others used caroling as an excuse to visit neighbors in a kind of moving holiday party. The singers here, though they proclaim themselves "neighbors' children" and not "daily beggars," still sing as though they're crashing a holiday party.

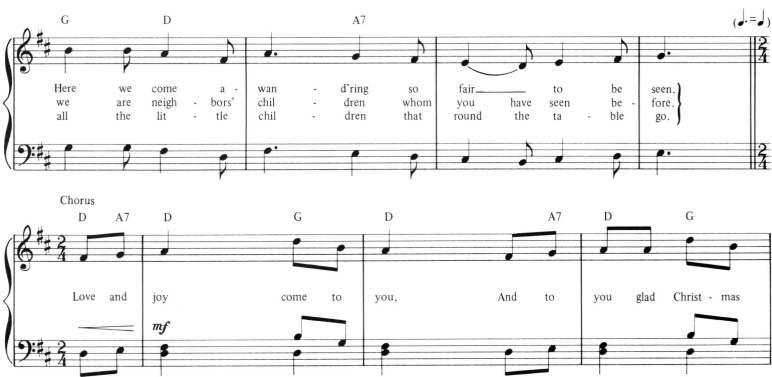

1. Here we come a-car-ol-ing a-mong the leaves so green;
(2.) are not dai-ly beg-gars that beg from door to door,
(3.) bless the mas-ter of this house, like-wise the mis-tress, too,

Here we come a-wan-d'ring so fair to be seen.
we are neigh-bors' chil-dren whom you have seen be-fore.
all the lit-tle chil-dren that round the ta-ble go.

But
And

Chorus

Love and joy come to you, And to you glad Christ-mas

(continued on page 37)

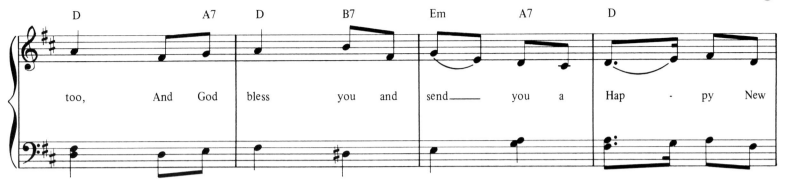

too, And God bless you and send_____ you a Hap - py New

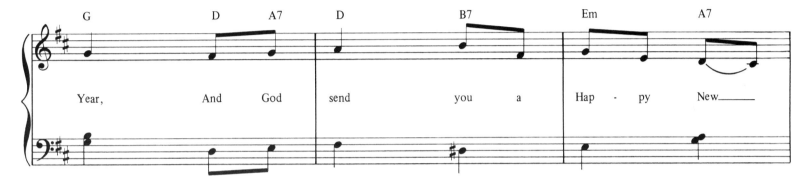

Year, And God send you a Hap - py New_____

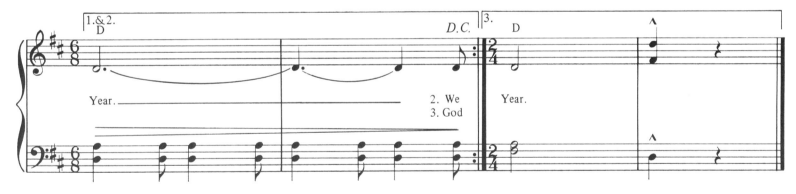

Year._____

D.C.

2. We
3. God

Year.

At left: *Central Park in Winter* (detail).
Published by Currier and Ives, American,
1857–1907.

At right: Details of illustrations in *Vieilles
chansons pour les petits enfants.*
Maurice Boutet de Monvel, French,
1851–1913.

37

I Saw Three Ships

English traditional

The image of three sailing ships probably comes from the twelfth century, when the supposed relics of the three Wise Men traveled by ship from Constantinople to Milan and finally to Cologne, where they eventually came to rest in the cathedral. This carol has been sung in many variations for at least five centuries, and over the years the voyagers became members of the Holy Family and the ships' destination became land-locked Bethlehem.

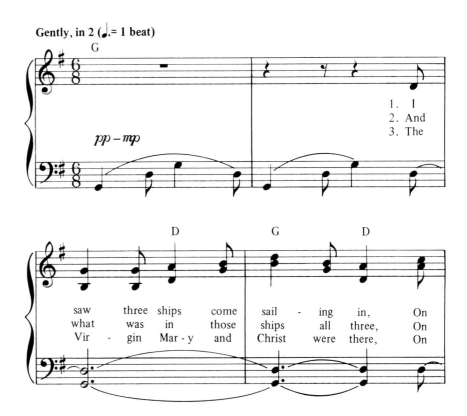

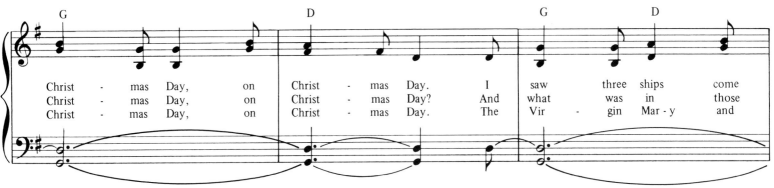

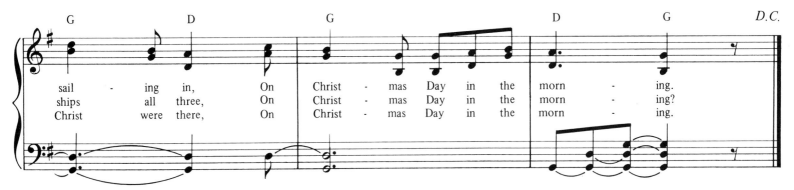

I Saw Three Ships (detail). Francis D. Bedford, British, 1864–1934.

The Annunciation to the Shepherds (detail). Henri Rivière, French, 1864–1951.

It Came Upon the Midnight Clear

Words by Edmund Hamilton Sears
Music by Richard Storrs Willis

The splendor of the angels and their message of peace on earth are vividly conveyed in this nineteenth-century carol. It is said that the author, a Massachusetts minister, wrote the words on a December day while snow was falling outside his study window. Like the song, Rivière's print re-creates the atmosphere of the silent, starlit night that is suddenly filled with the voices of angels.

1. It came up-on the mid-night clear, that
   glo - ri - ous song of old, From

2. Still through the clo - ven skies they come, with
   peace - ful wings un - furl'd; And

*Guitar: Capo 3rd fret

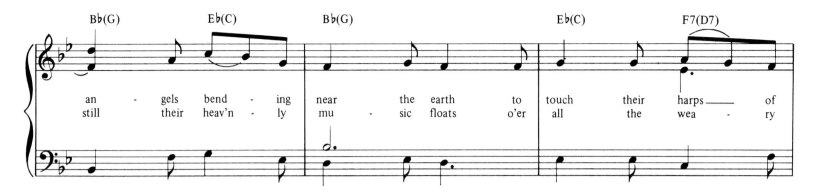

an - gels bend - ing near the earth to touch their harps ___ of
still their heav'n - ly mu - sic floats to o'er all the wea - ry

gold. ___ Peace on the earth, ___ good will to men from
world: ___ A - bove its sad ___ and low - ly plains from they

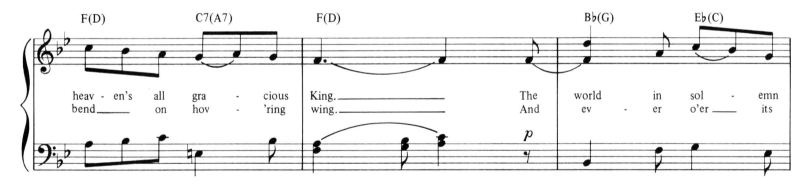

heav - en's all gra - cious King. ___ The world in sol - emn
bend ___ on hov - 'ring wing. ___ And ev - er o'er ___ its

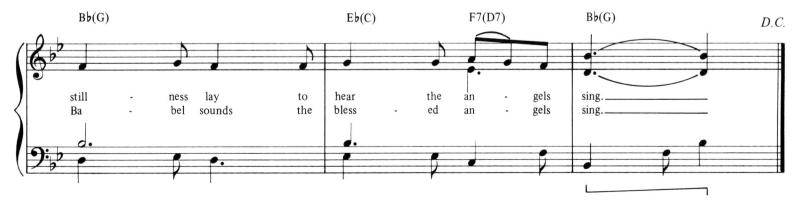

still - ness lay to hear the an - gels sing. ___
Ba - bel sounds to the bless - ed an - gels sing. ___

D.C.

41

Jingle Bells

Words and music by James Pierpont

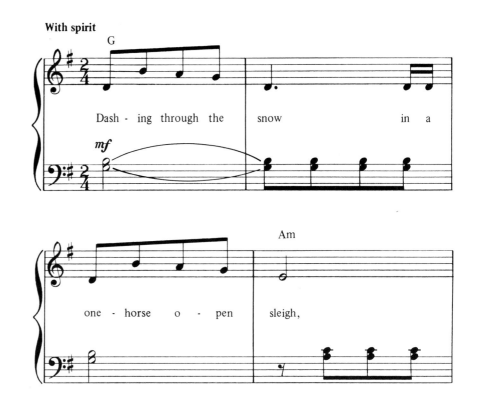

This most familiar of secular Christmas songs doesn't even mention Christmas, and in fact it was written for a Boston Sunday school to sing on Thanksgiving. The sleigh and bells make us think about Santa Claus, though, and the jaunty tune and jolly lyrics conjure up a nostalgic image of winter in bygone days. In this Currier and Ives print, the sleigh bells are clearly visible on the horses' harnesses.

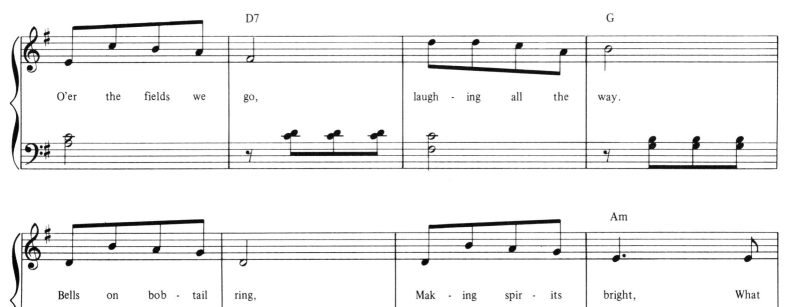

The Sleigh Race (detail). Published by Currier and Ives, American, 1857–1907.

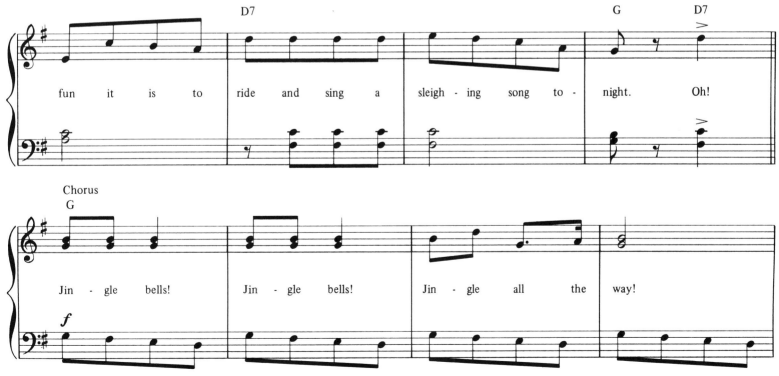

fun it is to ride and sing a sleigh-ing song to-night. Oh!

Jin-gle bells! Jin-gle bells! Jin-gle all the way!

(continued on page 44)

43

Jingle Bells

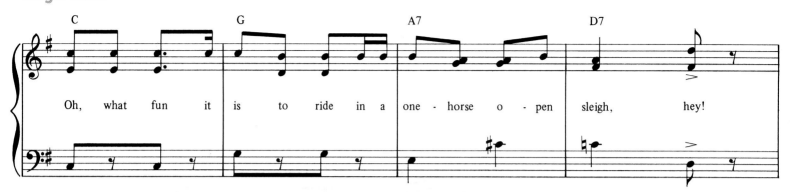

Oh, what fun it is to ride in a one-horse o-pen sleigh, hey!

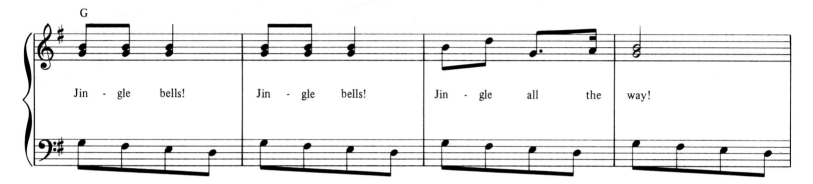

Jin - gle bells! Jin - gle bells! Jin - gle all the way!

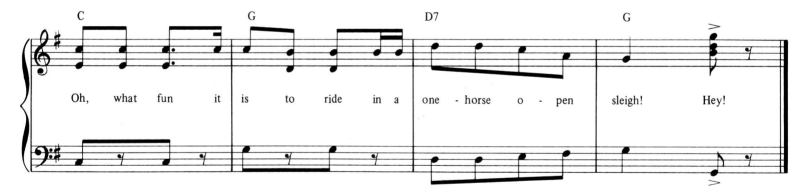

Oh, what fun it is to ride in a one-horse o-pen sleigh! Hey!

A Ride to School (detail). Published by Currier and Ives, American, 1857–1907.

Joy to the World

Words by Isaac Watts
Music by Lowell Mason

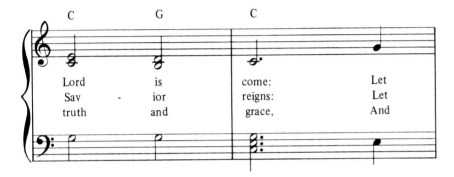

"Make a joyful noise unto the Lord, all the earth." These words from Psalm 98 inspired the author to write "Joy to the World" in 1719. It is easy to imagine angels, depicted by artists of the Italian Renaissance or the Harlem Renaissance, lifting their voices in a song like this one.

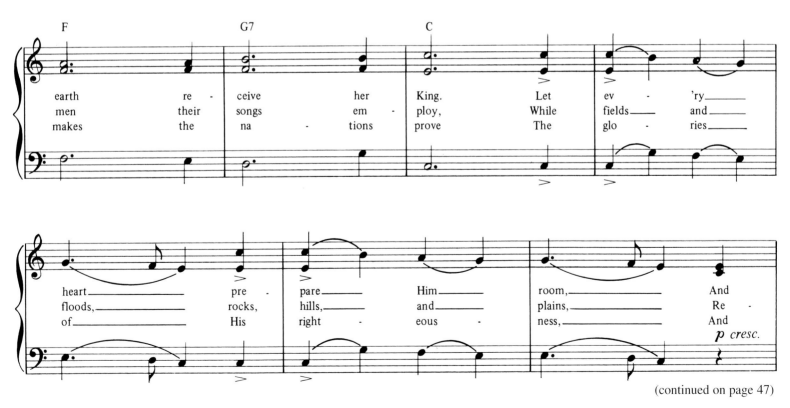

(continued on page 47)

heav'n and na - ture___ sing, and__ heav'n and na - ture___
peat the sound - ing__ joy, re - peat the sound - ing__
won - ders sound of His__ love, and__ won - ders sound of His__

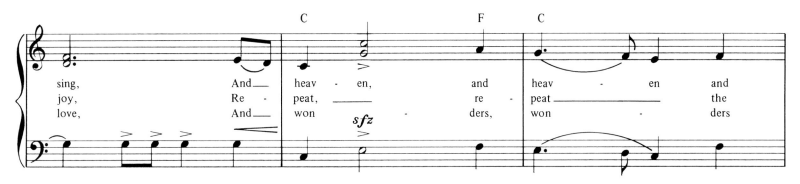

sing, And heav - en, and heav - en and
joy, Re - peat, __ re - peat __ the
love, And__ won - ders, won - ders

sfz

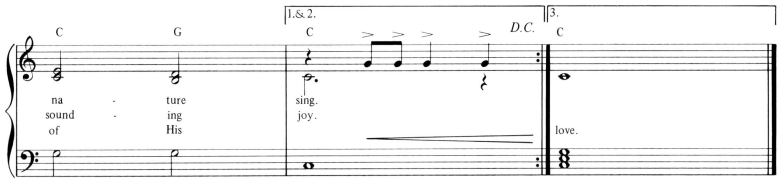

na - ture sing.
sound - ing joy.
of His love.

At left: *The Block* (detail).
Romare Bearden, American,
1911–1988.

At right: *Tungous Leaving
Their Winter Encampment*
(detail). Etched and pub-
lished by Adam & Gros,
after E. Karneyeff, Russian,
early 19th century.

O Christmas Tree

German traditional

The tradition of the Christmas tree has its roots in Germany, and there is historical evidence that Christmas trees were known there by 1605, but a popular legend tells that they began earlier, with Martin Luther. The German religious reformer, it is said, was inspired to decorate a tree with candles after he glimpsed the starry sky through some branches while walking through the woods on Christmas Eve.

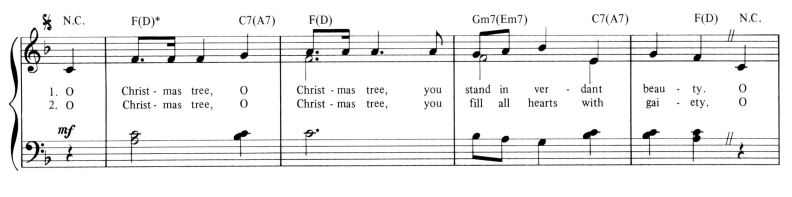

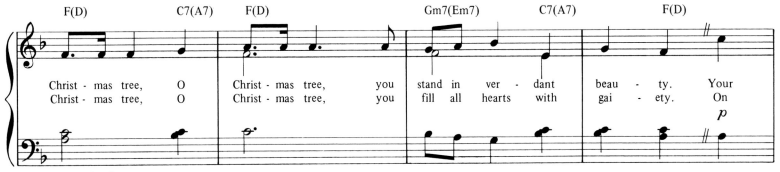

| | F(D)* | C7(A7) | F(D) | | Gm7(Em7) | C7(A7) | F(D) | N.C. |

1. O Christ - mas tree, O Christ - mas tree, you stand in ver - dant beau - ty. O
2. O Christ - mas tree, O Christ - mas tree, you fill all hearts with gai - ety. O

| F(D) | C7(A7) | F(D) | | Gm7(Em7) | C7(A7) | F(D) |

Christ - mas tree, O Christ - mas tree, you stand in ver - dant beau - ty. Your
Christ - mas tree, O Christ - mas tree, you fill all hearts with gai - ety. On

*Guitar: Capo 3rd fret

48

Snow-laden Pines (detail). Rockwell Kent, American, 1882–1971.

Christmas Eve Church (detail). Jeanne Kerremans, Belgian, active 1930s.

Moderately

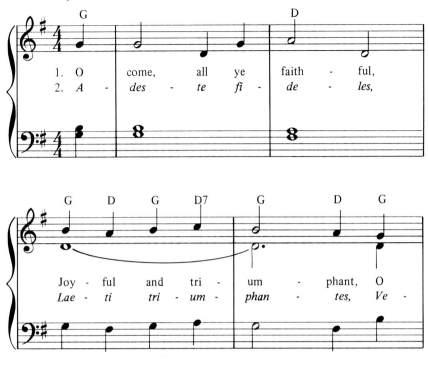

O Come, All Ye Faithful

Words by Frederick Oakeley (English)
and John Frances Wade (Latin)
Music by John Reading

Unlike some carols that incorporate a line or two in a foreign language, "Adeste Fideles" was originally written entirely in Latin. Several translations have been attempted over the years. Often sung as a processional hymn at Christmas services, this carol recalls the shepherds, the Wise Men, and the townsfolk who came to see the babe lying in a manger.

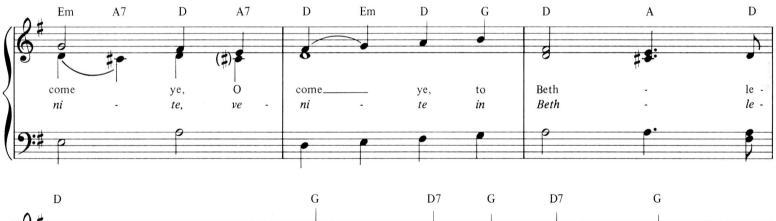

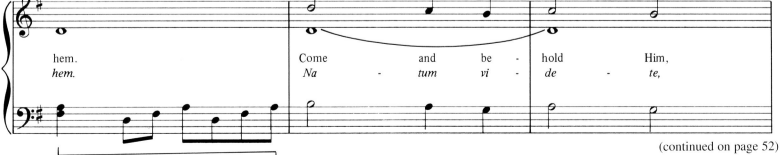

(continued on page 52)

O Come, All Ye Faithful

born the King of an - gels. O come, let us a -
Re - gem an - ge - lo - rum. Ve - ni - te a - do -

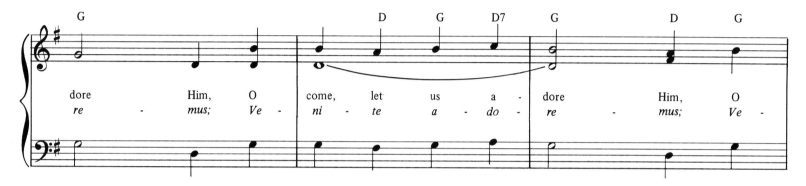

dore Him, O come, let us a - dore Him, O
re - mus; Ve - ni - te a - do - re - mus; Ve -

come, let us a - dore Him,_____ Christ_____ the Lord.
ni - te a - do - re - mus,_____ Do - mi - num.

Additional verses:

3. Sing, choirs of angels,
   Sing in exultation;
   Sing all ye citizens of heav'n above:
   Glory to God in the highest.
   O come, let us adore Him,
   O come, let us adore Him,
   O come, let us adore Him, Christ, the Lord.

4. Yea, Lord, we greet Thee,
   Born this happy morning;
   Jesus, to Thee be glory giv'n;
   Word of the Father, now in flesh appearing.
   O come, let us adore Him,
   O come, let us adore Him,
   O come, let us adore Him, Christ, the Lord.

O Holy Night

Words by John Sullivan Dwight
Music by Adolphe Adam

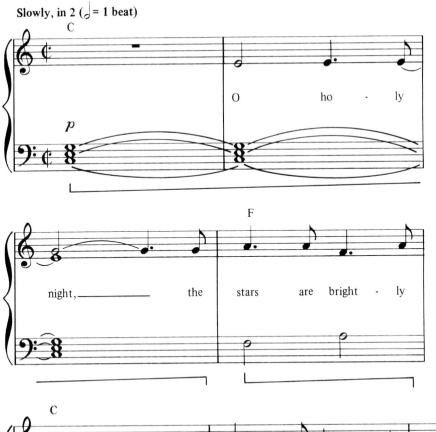

While the English words of this carol celebrate the entire night of Jesus' nativity, the original French version begins "Minuit, chrétiens," specifying to Christians that midnight was the actual, solemn hour of the Lord's birth. It is a very old belief that Jesus was born on the stroke of twelve, an idea that exists today in the tradition of midnight mass. This carol has an unusually operatic feel; the author was a composer of ballet and light opera.

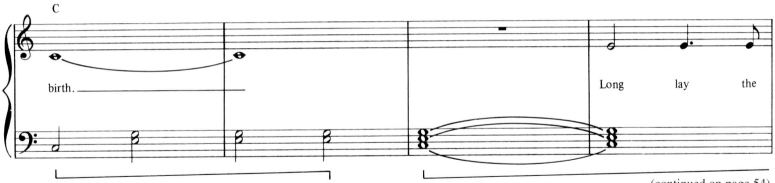

(continued on page 54)

O Holy Night

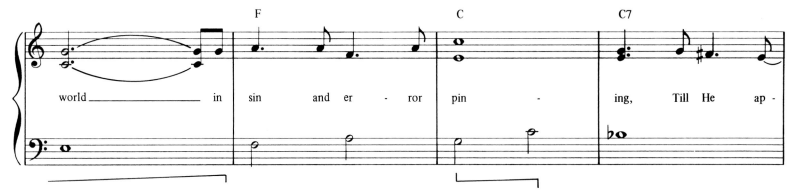

world ___ in sin and er - ror pin - ing, Till He ap-

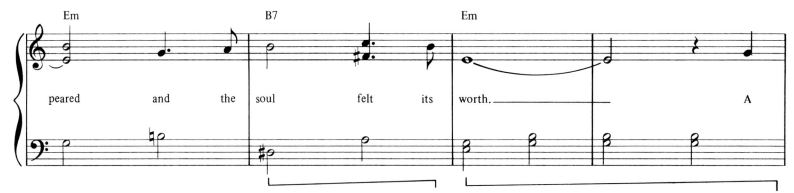

peared and the soul felt its worth. ___ A

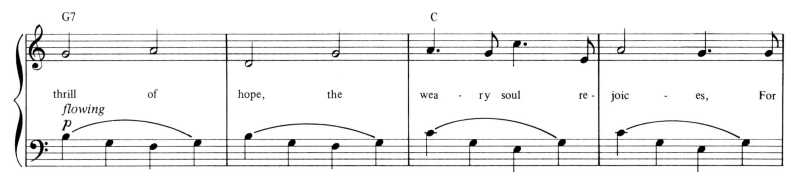

thrill of hope, the wea - ry soul re - joic - es, For

flowing
p

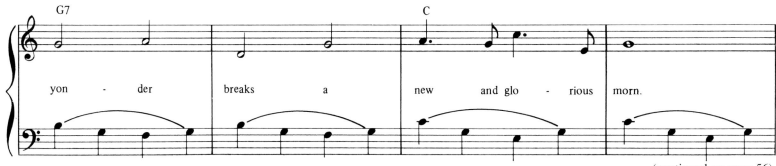

yon - der breaks a new and glo - rious morn.

(continued on page 56)

The Adoration of the Christ Child (detail). Follower of Jan Joest of Kalkar, Netherlandish, active about 1515.

Detail of a postcard. Franz Karl Delavilla, Austrian, 1884–1967.

O Holy Night

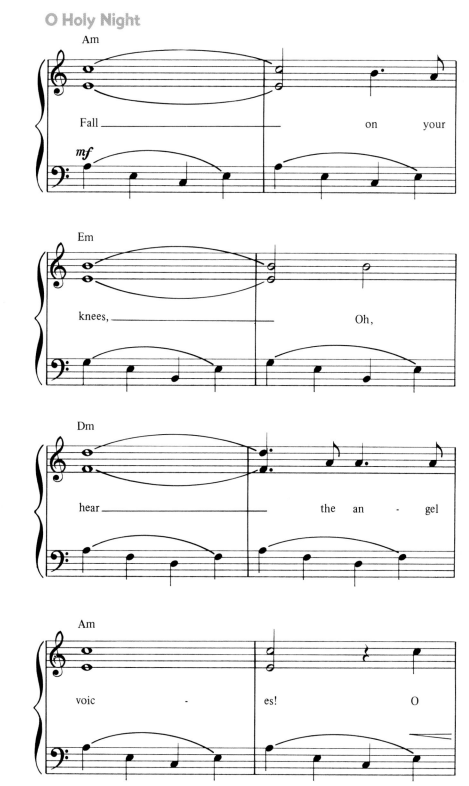

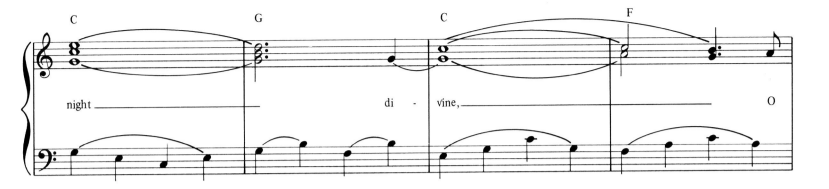

night _____ di - vine, _____ O

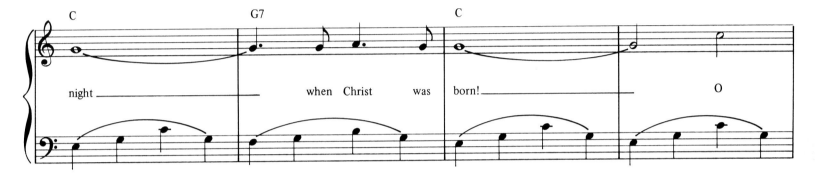

night _____ when Christ was born! _____ O

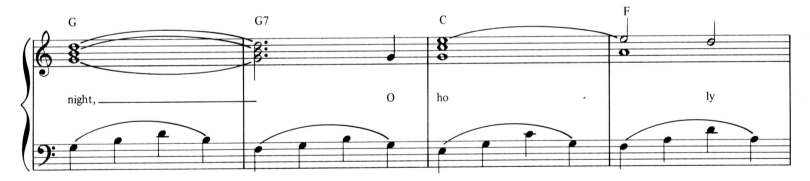

night, _____ O ho - ly

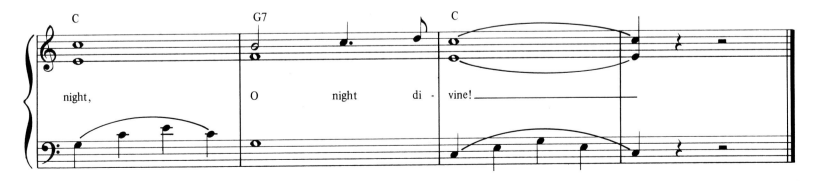

night, _____ O night di - vine! _____

O Little Town of Bethlehem

Words by Phillips Brooks
Music by Lewis H. Redner

In 1865, Phillips Brooks rode from Jerusalem to Bethlehem at Christmastime. Stopping in the field where the annunciation to the shepherds is supposed to have taken place, he watched night fall over the quiet village of Christ's birth. Later, he wrote these lyrics and gave them to his church organist, who woke up in the night with the idea for the melody.

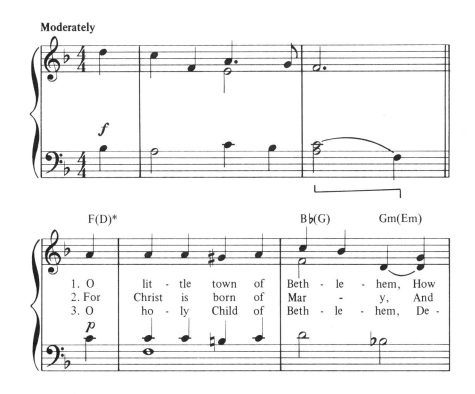

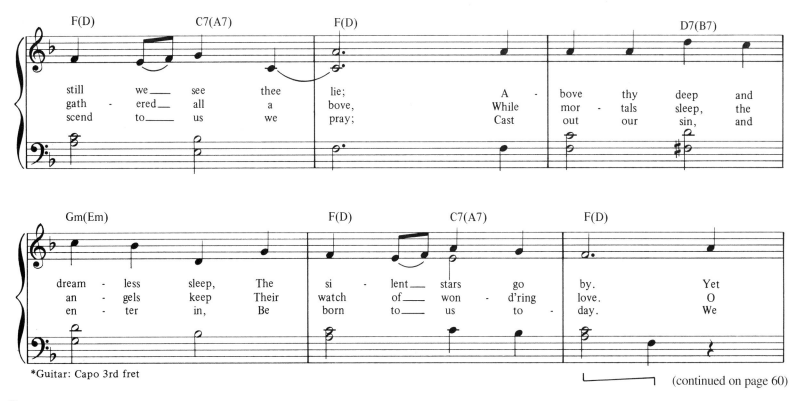

1. O lit - tle town of Beth - le - hem, How still we see thee lie; A - bove thy deep and dream - less sleep, The si - lent stars go by. Yet
2. For Christ is born of Mar - y, And gath - ered all a - bove, While mor - tals sleep, the an - gels keep Their watch of won - d'ring love. O
3. O ho - ly Child of Beth - le - hem, De - scend to us we pray; Cast out our sin, and en - ter in, Be born to us to - day. We

*Guitar: Capo 3rd fret

(continued on page 60)

The Arrival in Bethlehem (detail). Attributed to Master LC, Netherlandish, active second quarter 16th century.

O Little Town of Bethlehem

Virgin and Child (detail). Joos van Cleve and a collaborator,
Netherlandish, active by 1507, died 1540/41.

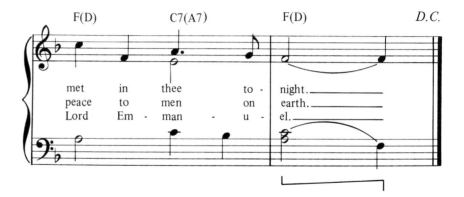

Santa Claus Is Comin' to Town

Words by Haven Gillespie
Music by J. Fred Coots

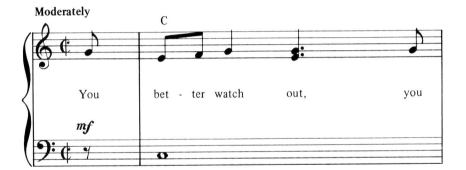

In spite of many claims, nobody has ever actually seen Santa Claus, and his appearance and habits have been the subjects of much speculation by various experts. Clement C. Moore, in his poem "A Visit from St. Nicholas," conjectured about Santa's sleigh and reindeer; cartoonist Thomas Nast was the first to suggest that he kept a list of the naughty and the nice.

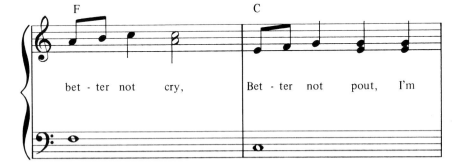
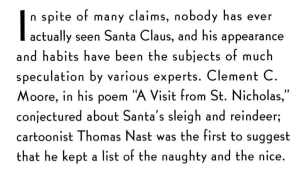

You better watch out, you better not cry, Better not pout, I'm

tell-ing you why: San-ta Claus is com-in' to town.

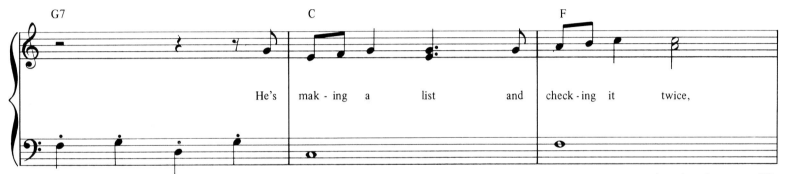

He's mak-ing a list and check-ing it twice,

(continued on page 62)

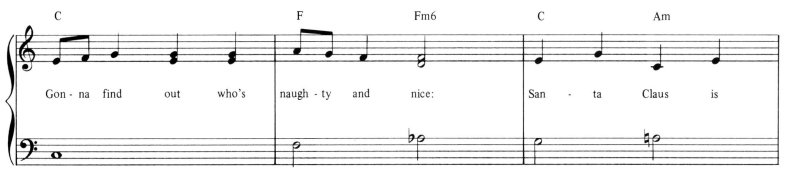

Gon - na find out who's naugh - ty and nice: San - ta Claus is

com - in' to town. He sees you when you're

sleep - in', He knows when you're a - wake. He knows if you've been

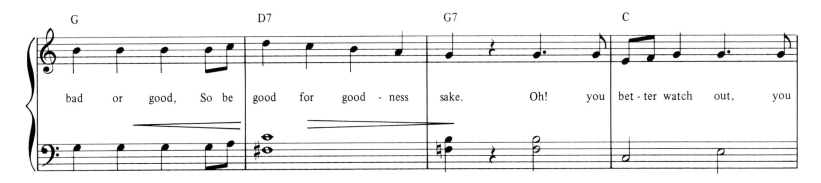

bad or good, So be good for good - ness sake. Oh! you bet - ter watch out, you

bet -ter not cry, Bet -ter not pout, I'm tell -ing you why:

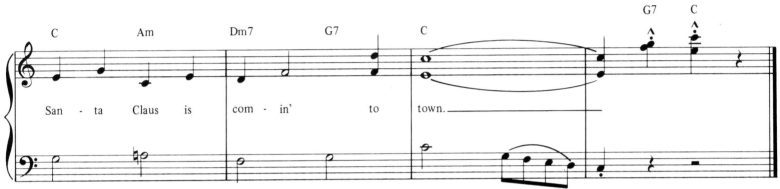

San - ta Claus is com - in' to town._____

Santa Claus in His Sleigh.
American, ca. 1880–1905.

Silent Night

Words adapted from the German
by Joseph Mohr
Music by Franz Grüber

Joseph Mohr, the young assistant pastor of St. Nicholas Church in Oberndorf, Austria, wrote the poem "Stille Nacht, Heilige Nacht." On Christmas Eve in 1818, he gave it to his organist, Franz Grüber, who composed the music, originally for guitar, in just a few hours. That very evening this enchanting song was sung at midnight mass.

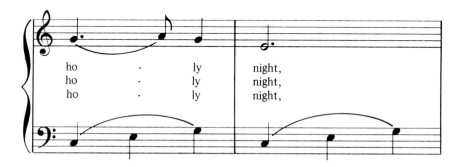

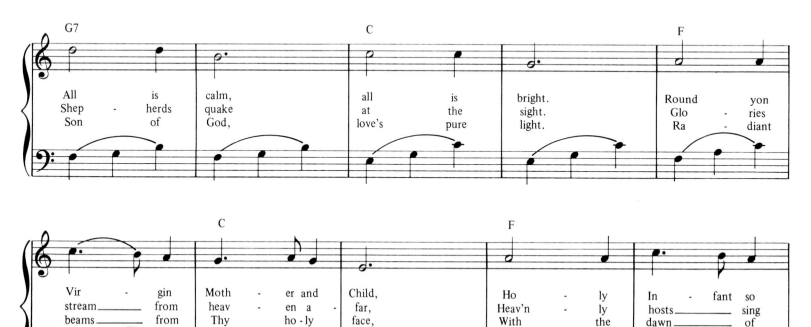

(continued on page 66)

The Way Home (detail). Ludwig Michaelek, Austrian, 1859–1942.

Asleep (detail). Horace Pippin, American, 1888–1946.

Silent Night

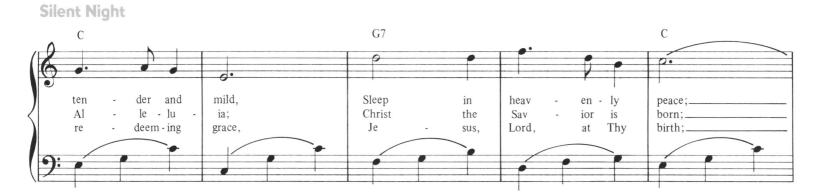

ten - der and	mild,	Sleep	in	heav - en - ly	peace;
Al - le - lu - ia;		Christ	the	Sav - ior is	born;
re - deem - ing grace,		Je - sus,	Lord,	at Thy	birth;

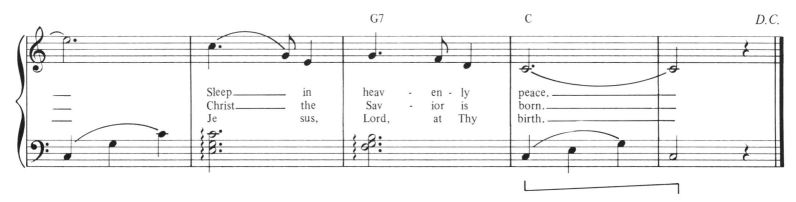

Sleep	in	heav - en - ly	peace.
Christ	the	Sav - ior is	born.
Je - sus,	Lord,	at Thy	birth.

Toyland

Words by Glen MacDonough
Music by Victor Herbert

The 1903 operetta "Babes in Toyland," about two children who escape from their evil uncle into a world of nursery rhyme characters and marching toys, was a spectacular show with elaborate sets and a cast of thousands. This dreamy and rather poignant song conjures up a magical world for children that is filled with all the treasures they might hope to find under the tree on Christmas morning.

*Guitar: Capo 3rd fret

(continued on page 68)

Toyland

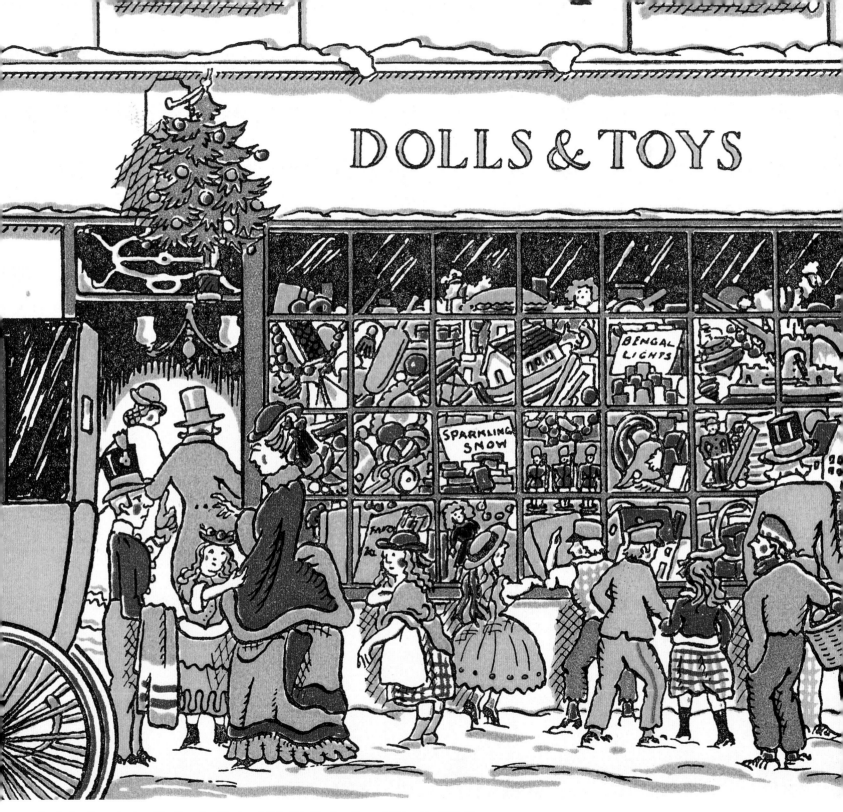

Detail of an illustration from *The Mysterious Toyshop, A Fairy Tale*. Wyndham Payne, British, active 1920–30.

Detail of a coverlet.
Sarah Furman
Warner Williams,
American, born
1760s, died ?

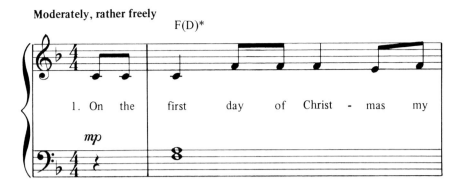

The Twelve Days of Christmas

English traditional

The twelve days of Christmas last from December 26 until January 6, the day that commemorates the gifts of the three Wise Men. This song certainly celebrates gift giving. The "pear tree" probably comes from the French word *perdrix* meaning "partridge," and the "five golden rings" may have originally been "five goldspinks" (goldfinches) or may have meant five ring-necked pheasants, either way sustaining the bird-related gifts for the first seven days.

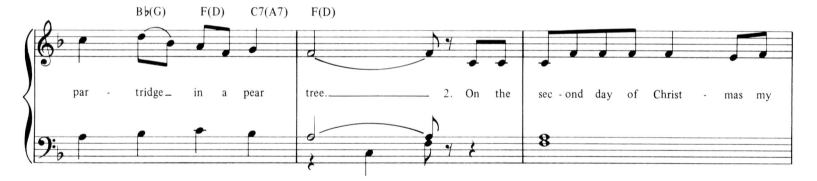

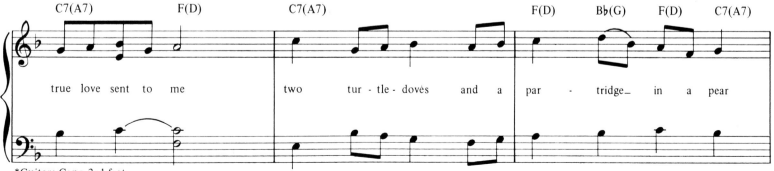

*Guitar: Capo 3rd fret

(continued on page 72)

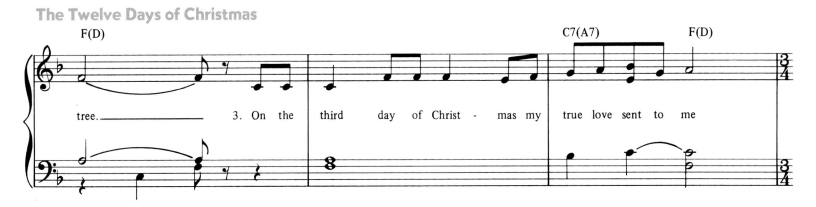

Marriage at Cana (detail). Anders Pålsson, Swedish, 1781–1849.

par - tridge in a pear tree. 5. On the fifth day of Christ - mas my

Broadly

true love sent to me five gold - en rings,

Briskly, as before

four call - ing birds,

three French hens, two turtle - doves, and a par - tridge in a pear tree. 6. On the

(continued on page 74)

The Twelve Days of Christmas

Detail of a postcard.
Rudolf Kalvack, Austrian,
1883–1932.

The Journey of the Magi (detail). Sassetta (Stefano di Giovanni), Italian (Sienese), active by 1423, died 1450.

We Three Kings

Words and music by John Henry Hopkins

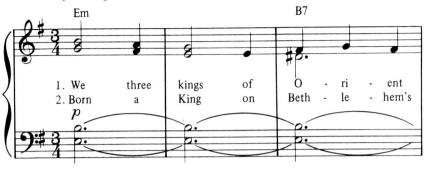

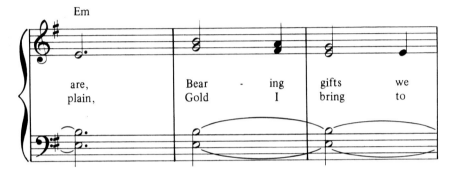

The Bible never mentions how many Wise Men visited the Christ child, but since they offered three gifts, it has become traditional to think that there were three of them. Gold was an appropriate gift for the King of Kings. Frankincense, its fragrant smoke required in many religious rituals, was believed to be pleasing to God. And myrrh, used as a balm for wounds and in burial rites, foretold Jesus' suffering and sacrifice.

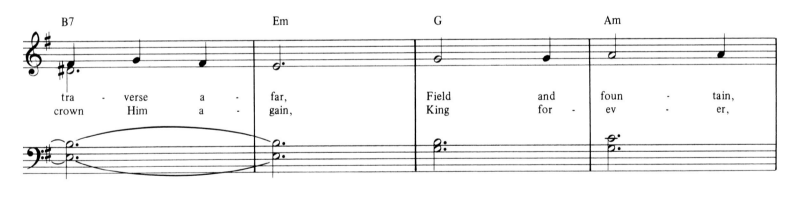

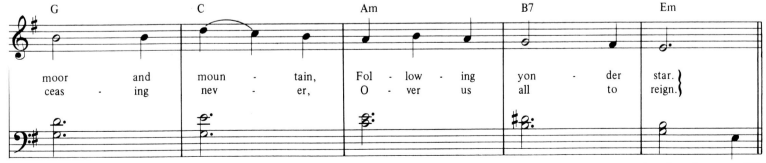

(continued on page 78)

We Three Kings

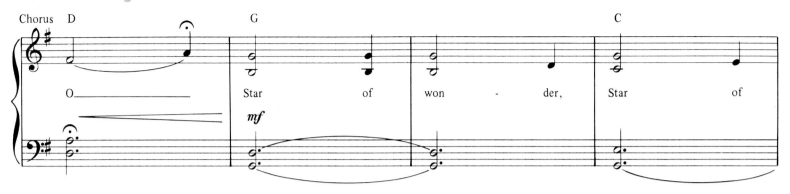

O_____ Star of won - der, Star of

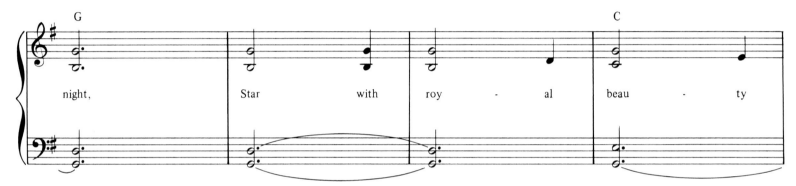

night, Star with roy - al beau - ty

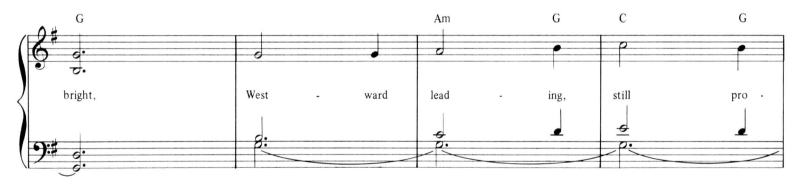

bright, West - ward lead - ing, still pro -

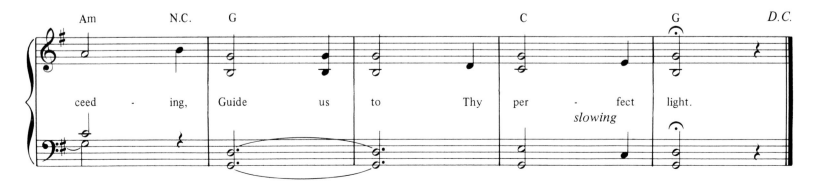

ceed - ing, Guide us to Thy per - fect light.

Additional verses:

3. Frankincense to offer have I,
   Incense owns a Deity nigh.
   Pray'r and praising, all men raising,
   Worship Him, God most high.
   (Chorus)

4. Myrrh is mine, its bitter perfume
   Breathes a life of gathering gloom;
   Sorrowing, sighing, bleeding, dying,
   Sealed in the stone-cold tomb.
   (Chorus)

5. Glorious now behold him arise,
   King and God and sacrifice.
   Alleluia, Alleluia,
   Earth to heav'ns replies.
   (Chorus)

The Adoration of the Magi (detail).
Workshop of Gerard David, Netherlandish,
born about 1455, died 1523.

We Wish You a
Merry Christmas

English traditional

The figgy pudding requested in this English carol is probably, in fact, plum pudding by another name. This traditional Christmas dessert contains neither plums nor figs; though it was originally sweetened with dried plums, it has long been made with raisins. In parts of England, raisins used to be called "figs," giving the dish another misleading name. Nowadays, it's generally just known as Christmas pudding.

Joyfully

1. We wish you a Mer - ry Christ - mas, We
2. Oh, bring us a fig - gy pud - ding, Oh,
3. We won't go un - til we've got some, We

wish you a Mer - ry Christ - mas, We
bring us a fig - gy pud - ding, Oh,
won't go un - til we've got some, We

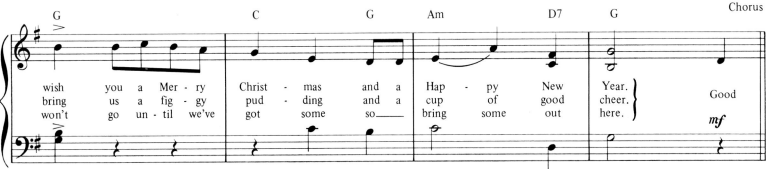

wish you a Mer - ry Christ - mas and a Hap - py New Year.
bring us a fig - gy pud - ding and a cup of good cheer.
won't go un - til we've got some so bring some out here.

Good

Chorus

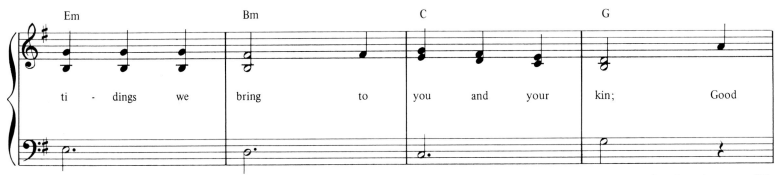

ti - dings we bring to you and your kin; Good

(continued on page 82)

Thanksgiving Turkey (detail). Anna Mary Robertson Moses (called Grandma Moses), American, 1860–1961.

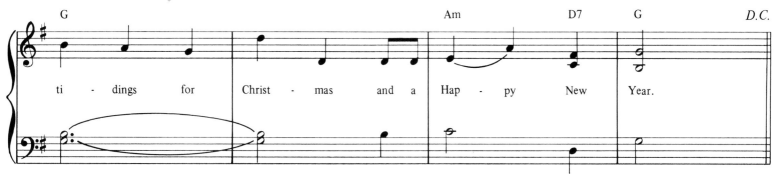

G   Am   D7   G   *D.C.*

ti - dings for Christ - mas and a Hap - py New Year.

Last time only

D7   G   C   E7   A7   D7

We wish you a Mer - ry Christ - mas, We wish you a Mer - ry Christ - mas, We

f

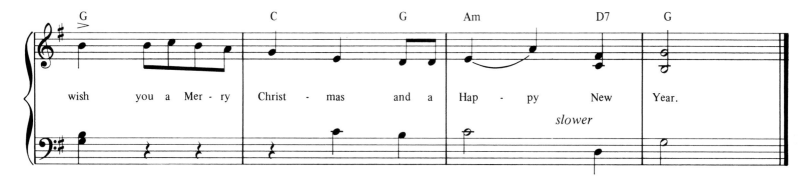

G   C   G   Am   D7   G

wish you a Mer - ry Christ - mas and a Hap - py New Year.

slower

Christmas Train. William H. Bradley, American, 1868–1964.

What Child Is This?

Words by William Chatterton Dix
Music English traditional

The ballad "Greensleeves" was probably already well known by 1580 when it was first licensed for printing, and it was familiar enough that by the end of the century it was mentioned twice by Shakespeare. Over the years, various lyrics have been sung to its haunting melody; these words were written in about 1865 by a Victorian hymnwriter and insurance company executive.

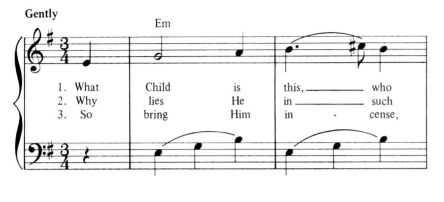

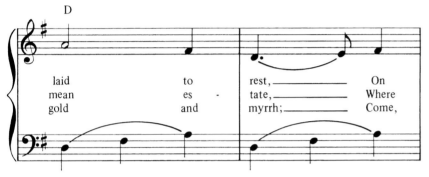

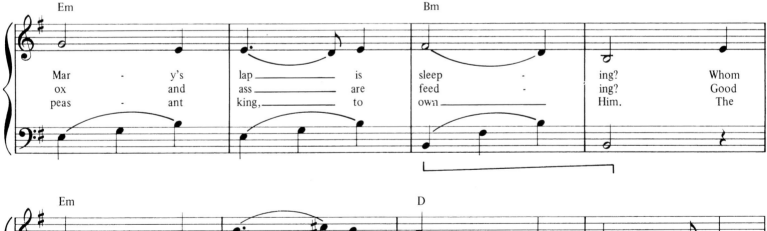

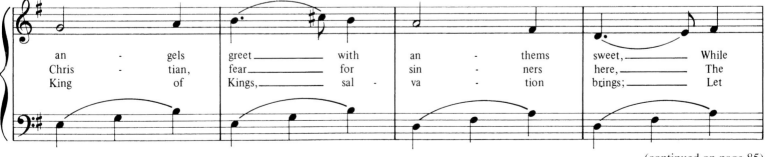

Gently

Em
1. What Child is this, _____ who
2. Why lies He in _____ such
3. So bring Him in - cense,

D
laid to rest, _____ On
mean es - tate, _____ Where
gold and myrrh; _____ Come,

Em   Bm
Mar - y's lap _____ is sleep - ing? Whom
ox and ass _____ are feed - ing? Good
peas - ant king, _____ to own _____ Him. The

Em   D
an - gels greet _____ with an - thems sweet, _____ While
Chris - tian, fear _____ for sin - ners here, _____ The
King of Kings, _____ sal - va - tion brings; _____ Let

(continued on page 85)

*Virgin and Child with the Young Saint
John the Baptist and Angels.* François
Boucher, French, 1703–1770.

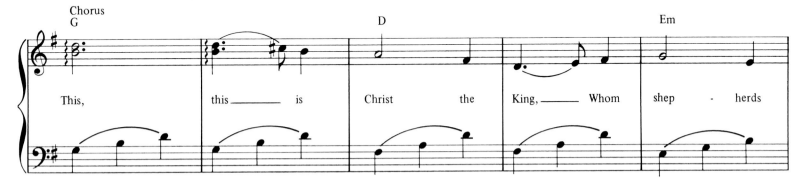

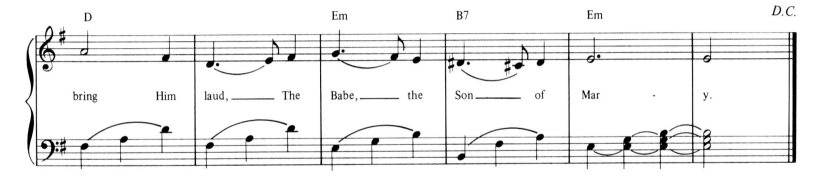

Credits

Page 7:
Detail of a postcard
Wiener Werkstätte, Austrian, founded 1905
Color lithograph, 5½ x 3½ in., 1908–14
Museum Accession, 1943   WW#169

Page 8:
Detail of a postcard
Carl Krenek, Austrian, 1880–1948
Color lithograph, 5½ x 3½ in., 1908–14
Museum Accession, 1943   WW#629

Page 11:
The Nativity (detail)
Gerard David, Netherlandish, ca. 1455–1523
Central panel of a triptych; oil on canvas, transferred from wood, 35½ x 28 in.
The Jules Bache Collection, 1949   49.7.20b

Pages 12–13:
Angel (detail)
Aubrey Beardsley, British, 1872–1898
Detail of a border design for *Le Morte d'Arthur* by Sir Thomas Malory, 1893–94
Drawing in black ink over traces of graphite on paper, 11⅛ x 8¾ in.
Rogers Fund, 1923   23.90

Page 15:
Central Park, Winter: The Skating Pond (detail)
Published by Currier and Ives, American, 1857–1907; designed by Charles Parsons, American, 1821–1910
Hand-colored lithograph, 18⅛ x 26⅝ in., ca. 1861
Bequest of Adele S. Colgate, 1962   63.550.266

Page 17:
The Nativity (detail)
German, Boppard-on-the-Rhine, Carmelite Church, 1445
Stained-glass panel, 41½ x 28½ in.
Francis L. Leland Fund, 1913   13.64.4

Page 19:
Scribner's for Xmas (detail)
Louis Rhead, American, 1857–1926
Commercial lithograph, 17⅛ x $9\frac{3}{16}$ in., 1895
Leonard A. Lauder Collection of American Posters, Gift of Leonard A. Lauder, 1984   1984.1202.147

Page 20:
Crèche figures: Nativity with angels and cherubs
Italian (Neapolitan), late 18th–early 19th century
Polychromed terracotta and wood, with silk garments
Gift of Loretta Hines Howard, 1964   64.164.1–.167

Page 22:
Praise of Music (detail)
Johannes Stradanus, Netherlandish, 1523–1605
From *Encomium Musices*, engraved by Adriaen Collaert, Netherlandish, ca. 1560–1618; engraving, $8\frac{9}{16}$ x 11 in.
The Elisha Whittelsey Collection, The Elisha Whittelsey Fund, 1949   49.95.995(2)

Page 23:
The Nativity (detail)
German, third quarter 15th century
Altar frontal with scenes from the life of the Virgin; wool, silk, and metal thread on linen warp, 3 ft. 5 in. x 11 ft. 6 in.
Gift of Charles F. Iklé, 1957   57.126

Page 25:
The Adoration of the Shepherds (detail)
Marcellus Coffermans, Netherlandish, active 1549–1570
Oil on wood, 8⅛ x 5½ in.
Gift of J. Pierpont Morgan, 1917   17.190.3

Page 26:
Christmas-Time, The Blodgett Family (detail)
Eastman Johnson, American, 1824–1906
Oil on canvas, 30 x 25 in., 1864
Gift of Mr. and Mrs. Stephen Whitney Blodgett, 1983   1983.486

Page 28:
Christmas Visitors (detail)
Randolph Caldecott, British, 1846–1886
From *Gleanings from the "Graphic,"* published in London, 1889; color woodcut, $10\frac{15}{16}$ x $14\frac{15}{16}$ in.
Gift of Juliet W. Robinson, 1918   18.77

Page 30:
Old King Cole (detail)
Francis D. Bedford, British, 1864–1934
From *A Book of Nursery Rhymes*, published in New York, 1897; color woodcut, 6⅜ x 4⅝ in.
The Elisha Whittelsey Collection, The Elisha Whittelsey Fund, 1966   66.540.2

Page 31:
End of the Hunt (detail)
Dale Nichols, American, 1904–1995
Oil on canvas, 30¼ x 40 in., 1934
Arthur Hoppock Hearn Fund, 1938   38.173

Page 33:
Madonna and Child with Saints (detail)
Girolamo dai Libri, Italian (Veronese), 1474–1555
Tempera and oil on canvas (arched top), 13 ft. 1 in. x 6 ft. 9½ in., ca. 1520
Fletcher Fund, 1920   20.92

Page 34:
Detail of a postcard
Wiener Werkstätte, Austrian, founded 1905
Color lithograph, 5½ x 3½ in., 1908–14
Museum Accession, 1943   WW#739

Page 36:
Central Park in Winter (detail)
Published by Currier and Ives, American, 1857–1907
Color lithograph, 8½ x 10½ in.
Bequest of Adele S. Colgate, 1962   63.550.337

Page 37:
Details of illustrations in *Vieilles chansons pour les petits enfants*
Maurice Boutet de Monvel, French, 1851–1913
Color lithograph, 1883
Gift of Mrs. John S. Lamont, 1974   1974.669

Page 39:
I Saw Three Ships (detail)
Francis D. Bedford, British, 1864–1934
From *A Book of Nursery Rhymes*, published in New York, 1897; color woodcut, 6⅜ x 4⅝ in.
The Elisha Whittelsey Collection, The Elisha Whittelsey Fund, 1966   66.540.2

Page 40:
The Annunciation to the Shepherds (detail)
Henri Rivière, French, 1864–1951
From a broadside for the book *La Marche à l'étoile* by Georges Fragerolle; color lithograph, 11⅜ x 16 in.
The Elisha Whittelsey Collection, The Elisha Whittelsey Fund, 1966   66.559.65

Page 43:
The Sleigh Race (detail)
Published by Currier and Ives, American, 1857–1907
Hand-colored lithograph, 9½ x 14½ in., 1859
Bequest of Adele S. Colgate, 1962   63.550.254

Page 44:
A Ride to School (detail)
Published by Currier and Ives, American, 1857–1907
Hand-colored lithograph, 5 x 8 in.
Bequest of Adele S. Colgate, 1962   63.550.356

Page 46:
The Block (detail)
Romare Bearden, American, 1911–1988
Cut and pasted papers on Masonite, 4 ft. x 18 ft., 1971
Gift of Mr. and Mrs. Samuel Shore, 1978   1978.61.2

Page 47:
Tungous Leaving Their Winter Encampment (detail)
Etched and published by Adam & Gros after E. Karneyeff, Russian, early 19th century
Color aquatint, 9¾ x 13⅝ in.
Louis V. Bell Fund, 1966   66.506.51

Page 49:
Snow-laden Pines (detail)
Rockwell Kent, American, 1882–1971
Textile design in gouache over pencil on board, ca. 1950
Purchase, Leon Lowenstein Foundation Inc. Gift, 1976   1976.536.7

Page 50:
Christmas Eve Church (detail)
Jeanne Kerremans, Belgian, active 1930s
From *Le Manteau du Roi et autres contes de Noël* by
Camille Melloy, published in Brussels, 1939;
color lithograph, 6⅛ x 6⅛ in.
Gift of C. Whitney Dall Jr., in memory of Emily M. Dall,
1976   1976.625.3

Page 55:
The Adoration of the Christ Child (detail)
Follower of Jan Joest of Kalkar, Netherlandish,
active about 1515
Oil on wood, 41 x 28¼ in.
The Jack and Belle Linsky Collection, 1982   1982.60.22

Page 56:
Detail of a postcard
Franz Karl Delavilla, Austrian, 1884–1967
Color lithograph, 5½ x 3½ in., 1908
Museum Accession, 1943   WW#19

Page 59:
The Arrival in Bethlehem (detail)
Attributed to Master LC, Netherlandish,
active second quarter 16th century
Oil on wood, 26½ x 36⅞ in., ca. 1540
Rogers Fund, 1916   16.69

Page 60:
Virgin and Child (detail)
Joos van Cleve and a collaborator, Netherlandish, active by
1507, died 1540/41
Oil on wood, 28⅜ x 21¼ in., ca. 1525
The Jack and Belle Linsky Collection, 1982   1982.60.47

Page 63:
Santa Claus in His Sleigh
American, ca. 1880–1905
Advertising card for Union Pacific Tea Co.;
color lithograph, 5 x 7 in.
The Jefferson R. Burdick Collection, Gift of Jefferson R.
Burdick, 1947   Album 19, page 9r

Page 65:
The Way Home (detail)
Ludwig Michaelek, Austrian, 1859–1942
Color etching, 9⅝ x 13⅝ in., 1901
Rogers Fund, 1923   23.52.12(4)

Page 66:
Asleep (detail)
Horace Pippin, American, 1888–1946
Oil on canvas board, 9 x 12 in., 1943
Bequest of Jane Kendall Gingrich, 1982   1982.55.3

Page 69:
Detail of an illustration from *The Mysterious Toyshop,
A Fairy Tale*
Wyndham Payne, British, active 1920–30
Published in London, 1924; color woodcut, 9 x 5⅝ in.
Rogers Fund, 1970   1970.544.1

Page 70:
Detail of a coverlet
Sarah Furman Warner Williams, American, born 1760s, died ?
Linen, with linen and cotton appliqués and silk embroidery
thread, 8 ft. 7¼ in. x 7 ft. 6½ in., ca. 1803
Gift of Catherine E. Cotheal, 1938   38.59

Page 73:
Marriage at Cana (detail)
Anders Pålsson, Swedish, 1781–1849
Painted linen, 29 in. x 12 ft. 7 in., 1818
Gift of Mr. and Mrs. William Maxwell Evarts, 1953   53.98

Page 75:
Detail of a postcard
Rudolf Kalvack, Austrian, 1883–1932
Color lithograph, 5½ x 3½ in., ca. 1908
Museum Accession, 1943   WW#15

Page 76:
The Journey of the Magi (detail)
Sassetta (Stefano di Giovanni), Italian (Sienese),
active by 1423, died 1450
Tempera and gold on wood, 8½ x 11¾ in., ca. 1435
Maitland F. Griggs Collection, Bequest of Maitland F. Griggs,
1943   43.98.1

Page 79:
The Adoration of the Magi (detail)
Workshop of Gerard David, Netherlandish, born about
1455, died 1523
Oil on wood, 27¾ x 28⅞ in., ca. 1520
The Jack and Belle Linsky Collection, 1982   1982.60.17

Page 81:
Thanksgiving Turkey (detail)
Anna Mary Robertson Moses (called Grandma Moses),
American, 1860–1961
Oil on wood, 15⅛ x 19⅛ in., 1943
Bequest of Mary Stillman Harkness, 1950   50.145.375

Page 82:
Christmas Train
William H. Bradley, American, 1868–1964
Graphite on tracing paper, 6½ x 14⅜ in., 1949
Gift of Fern Bradley Dufner, 1952   52.625.154

Page 84:
*Virgin and Child with the Young Saint John the Baptist and
Angels*
François Boucher, French, 1703–1770
Oil on canvas; oval, 16⅛ x 13⅝ in., 1765
Gift of Adelaide Milton de Groot, in memory of the
de Groot and Hawley families, 1966   66.167

Page 87:
Detail of a postcard
Mela Koehler, Austrian, 1885–1960
Color lithograph, 5½ x 3½ in., 1908–14
Museum Accession, 1943   WW#735

Page 88:
Detail of a postcard
Wiener Werkstätte, Austrian, founded 1905
Color lithograph, 5½ x 3½ in., 1908–14
Museum Accession, 1943   WW#168